BICYCLES AND BICYCLING

BICYCLES AND BICYCLING

BY GEORGE S. FICHTER

A FIRST BOOK

FRANKLIN WATTS
NEW YORK | LONDON | 1978

Photographs courtesy of:

Bicycle Manufacturers Association of America, Inc.: pp. 2, 6, 9, 10, 13, 14, 18, 19, 20, 24, 29 (top), 32, 34 (top), 41, 56; Schwinn Bicycle Company, Chicago: pp. 29 (bottom), 55; Meryl Joseph: p. 34 (bottom); Bicycle Institute of America, Inc.: p. 44.

Library of Congress Cataloging in Publication Data

Fichter, George S

Bicycles and bicycling.
(A First book)
Bibliography: p.
Includes index.
SUMMARY: Highlights the history of bicycles, discusses safety rules, presents guidelines for selecting and maintaining a bicycle, and offers suggestions for games, rides, and tours.

1. Bicycles and tricycles—Juvenile literature. 2. Cycling—Juvenile literature. [1. Bicycles and bicycling] I. Title.

GV1043.5.F5 796.6 77–16511
ISBN 0–531–01403–7

Printed in the United States of America
6 5 4 3 2

CONTENTS

BICYCLES AND BICYCLING

1 YOU AND YOUR BICYCLE

You can really go places on your bicycle. No more walking or waiting around for somebody to take you by car. If it takes you half an hour to walk to your friend's house, you can get there in five minutes on your bicycle.

When you have to run an errand, you can do it by bicycle in a hurry and have time left over for a game.

You can use your bicycle to earn money, too. Get a job making deliveries. With your bicycle you can also ride back and forth to jobs of all sorts—mowing lawns, baby-sitting, or whatever. Your bicycle makes you independent.

You can ride your bicycle to school, to the movies, to the park—and on Saturdays, you can explore the countryside for miles around. When the weather is right, you and your friends might even go on overnight bike hikes. A whole new world is yours when you have a bicycle.

You will not be alone on your bicycle. Millions of people around the world ride bicycles today, and more bicycles than automobiles are sold every year. Most people start with a

tricycle when they are very young, and they may also use trainer wheels for a while after they get their first two-wheeler. But balancing is really easy, almost automatic. And then the excitement begins.

Bicycling is fun, and it gets you where you want to go. It is also good for you. It uses a lot of muscles and keeps you in good shape. As an all-around conditioning exercise, only swimming rates higher. But you can't swim down to a shop for a loaf of bread or to a friend's house for a visit. You can ride your bicycle to the swimming pool, though, and get the benefit of both exercises. For whatever you want to do, a bicycle is always as ready to go as you are.

Bicycling is fun for everyone.

2

THE BICYCLE THROUGH HISTORY

Nobody really knows who invented the bicycle. A stained-glass window installed in a church in England in 1642 depicts a cherub straddling a wheeled vehicle that looks much like the earliest so-called "bicycles." Even older Egyptian art shows a similar kind of wheeled contraption. Most historians, however, now credit the invention of the bicycle to a Frenchman by the name of M. de Sivrac. In 1791, he mounted a wooden rail between two wheels, then sat on the rail and pushed with his feet. This contraption was called a *célérifère,* a French word that means "fast feet." There was no way of steering this vehicle, but it was great for going downhill or for rolling for short distances on smooth, level ground. No one got excited about this vehicle, however.

In 1816, Baron von Drais, a German forester, made an almost identical foot-pushed vehicle that did become quite popular in Europe. Called draisines, walkalongs, or hobby-horses, the earliest models could not be steered. To change direction, the rider stopped and turned the whole rig before setting off again. In later versions, the front wheel could be turned for steering. Some had wooden wheels, and others had iron wheels. Some were equipped with leather or cushioned seats, and in a few models, the seats were mounted on springy metal to help make the ride less bumpy. The tandems —pushed by two people—were said to go as fast as 6 miles (10 km) per hour on level ground! When they were rolling downhill, they passed horse-drawn carriages and caused startled horses to bolt.

PEDAL POWER

Inventors went to work immediately and soon came up with a primitive pedal mechanism for supplying power to the bicycle, but the interest in bicycles died down for a number of years. It was a Frenchman, Ernest Michaux, who is given credit for the first really successful pedal bicycle. The pedals were attached directly to the front wheel. Pierre Lallement, who had worked in Michaux's shop in France, went to the United States and got a patent on a very similar kind of vehicle in 1866.

In the Lallement bicycle, the front wheel was slightly larger than the rear wheel. The pedals were three-sided wooden wedges, and in later versions, they were weighted and were also on pivots to keep them in an up position as the wheel turned. Variations began to appear rapidly. In each

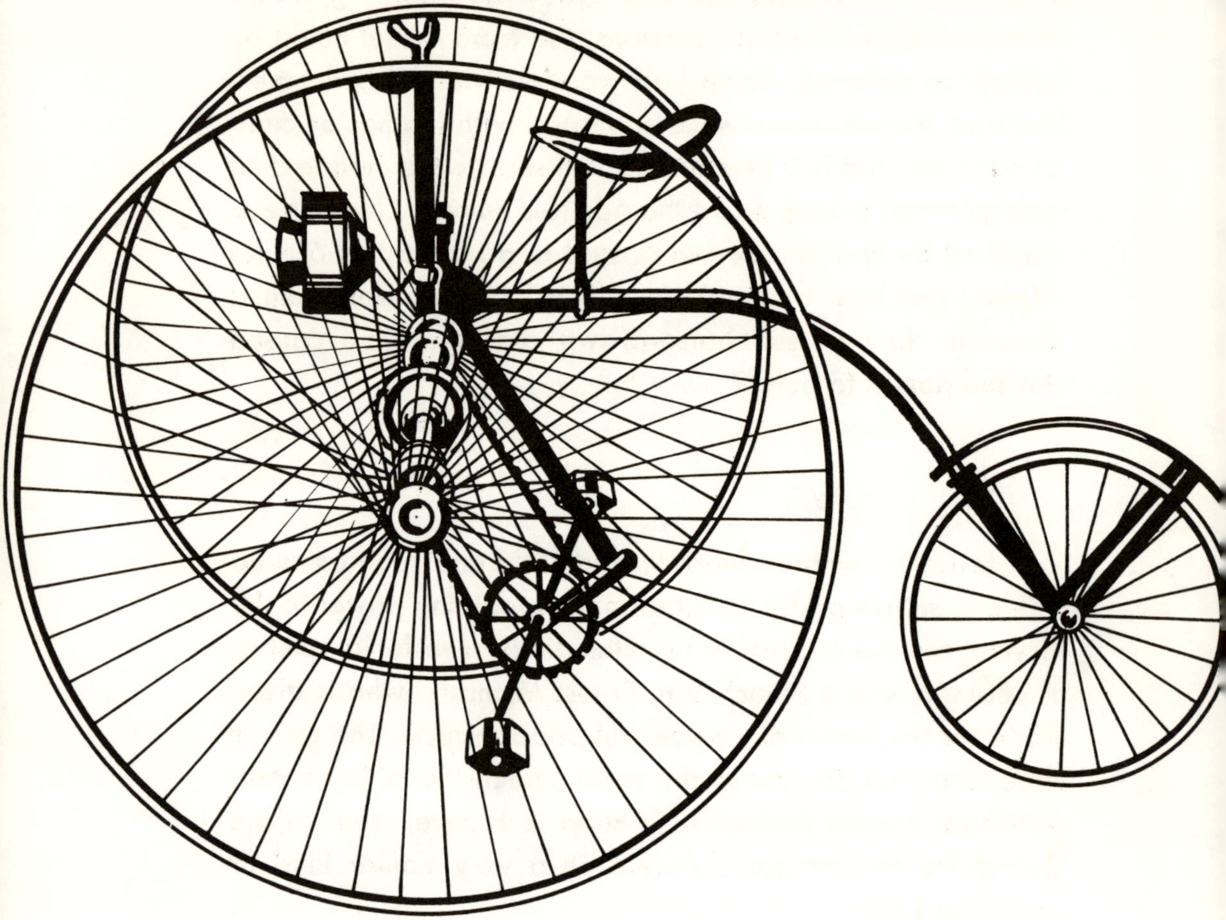

An 1878 tricycle

new style, the front wheel became a little larger, the rear wheel smaller. This was done because each revolution of the pedals sent the wheel revolving over a greater distance. In some of the largest, the front wheel was more than 5 feet (1½ m) tall. To get to the seat on top of these big wheels, riders had to mount their bicycles from a high perch. If they came to a hill that was too steep to pedal and had to dismount, they sometimes had to walk for miles, pushing their bicycle to find a place where they could get back on. A fall or "header" from a high-wheeler was dangerous.

Soon the big-wheeled bicycles, or "ordinaries," were equipped with a runglike step on the frame just above the rear wheel. Skilled riders could push a bicycle along the ground to get up speed and then quickly use this step to climb into the saddle. They had to start moving the pedals fast to keep the bicycle in motion. Speeds of 10 to 12 miles (12 to 20 km) per hour were not uncommon, and some bicyclists managed to get their machines up to 20 miles (32 km) per hour. Bicycles were unquestionably the fastest things on the roads during the mania for bicycles that swept the country during the late 1800s.

Many strange vehicles moved over the roads of America and Europe during those days. Some were even rowed like boats, the rider sitting in the middle with two big wheels on each side. To provide stability, many of the vehicles had three or even four wheels. An increase in the number of wheels meant a slower speed, of course, and the interest in getting around in a hurry kept most people on two-wheelers.

SAFETY BICYCLES

Because the high-wheeled bicycles were not safe—a small rock or a rut could make a big bike buck—inventors turned their attention toward creating a safer bicycle. They produced a bicycle with two wheels of almost equal size, very much like the first ones that were built. But these new "safety" bicycles had pedals. Soon sprockets and a chain drive were added. This increased the distance a wheel revolved with each turn of the pedals. In basic design these bicycles were much like those we ride today. And in the 1890s, a good bicycle cost almost the same as today, but at a time when that sum of money was much more difficult to come by. Millions of people nevertheless found the money, even depriving themselves of necessities to join in the craze for bicycling.

Bicycles also opened up many other avenues for inventors. It was bicycle manufacturers and repairers who produced the first automobiles and the first planes, borrowing both materials and ideas from bicycles for their inventions. These included pneumatic tires, brakes, freewheeling mechanisms, shaft drives, ball bearings, and other features. It was also the bicycle that changed the style of women's clothes from hoopskirts and other awkward, shackling garb to short skirts, bloomers, culottes, and other kinds of clothes that gave them freedom while riding and in getting on and off their bicycles.

An 1880 ordinary

TIMES
BIKE
TIMES
BIKE

SPEED ON WHEELS

In those days (and yet today), people were obsessed with speed. Bicycle races were popular from the start. They are still a major sport in Europe and are increasing in popularity in the United States. In the 1940s Alf Letourner, a famous six-day bicycle racer from France, achieved the phenomenal speed of 108.9 miles (175.2 km) per hour. This record was broken in 1962 by José Meiffret, also of France, who rode a bicycle down the Autobahn in Germany at 128 miles (205.9 km) per hour. No one thought this speed could ever be beaten. But in 1973, Dr. Al Abbott, an American, did 138.67 miles (223.12 km) per hour across the Utah salt flats. This is the top speed ever achieved by a human using only muscles for power.

In all of these speed records, the racers rode behind some sort of vehicle that served as a windbreak so that, in effect, they rode in a vacuum. Admittedly, these bicyclists could never have gone as fast without this help, but the performances are still incredible. They demonstrate not only muscle power but also human ingenuity in creating a mechanism that can be geared to take maximum advantage of this power.

This early bicycle was a home on wheels!

3 WHICH BICYCLE SHOULD YOU BUY?

Several basic styles of bicycles are available today. Each is good for a particular use, and you should select the kind that suits your needs best. All of the bicycles are available in models for both boys and girls. Growing in popularity is the so-called "mixte" bicycle, which has a frame about halfway between the standard for either boys or girls.

UTILITY BICYCLES

Utility bicycles have a heavy, sturdy frame and give a smooth ride even on bumpy roads. They can also carry heavy loads. If you carry newspapers, a utility bicycle is probably the kind you need. Most of them have a single speed and simple brakes. Utility bicycles are fine for riding to school or around the town. They can withstand a lot of abuse—more than a bicycle deserves—but they are not the best for taking long rides or for speed.

A utility bicycle

RECREATIONAL BICYCLES

Recreational bicycles are lightweights, and most of them have a gearing mechanism for three speeds. Many of them are very well made. Lightweight bicycles have tires with a smaller diameter than those on utility bicycles. They do not give as soft a ride on a rough road, but they are much easier to pedal and are faster. Most important, you can get this speed with less effort, or you can ride for a longer time without getting tired. If you do not need to carry heavy loads, this may be the kind of bicycle you need.

TOURING BICYCLES

Touring bicycles are probably the most popular today. They are also the most expensive of the types for general riding. These bicycles have very lightweight frames and typically have dropped or turned-under handlebars. They are equipped with derailleur gears, most of them with gear combinations that provide ten speeds. The ten-speed derailleur consists of two large sprockets by the pedals, attached to the cranks, and five small sprockets in a unit called the free-wheeling cluster attached to the rear wheel. With a shift lever, you can cause the chain to move from one sprocket to another. One lever controls the position of the chain on the

These two girls are riding touring bicycles with dropped handlebars.

front sprockets, and another changes the position of the chain on the rear sprocket. "Speeds" in bicycles actually refer to the number of gears or sprocket combinations possible.

When you change the gears or "speeds," you determine the amount of energy you must spend to turn the wheels. This affects your speed—but only secondarily. You actually select the most comfortable rate to pedal (60 to 65 revolutions per minute is best for most people) and then adjust the gears to be able to maintain this rate with the least effort. Changing the gears to find the best gear combination is called "twiddling."

When you are riding uphill or into the wind, you shift into a lower gear, that is, the chain on the smallest of the sprockets in front and one of the largest in the rear cluster. You will pedal at the same rate as before, but you move forward more slowly. When you are on level ground or when the wind is pushing at your back, you will shift into a higher gear. You will pedal at the same rate, spending no more energy but going much faster. Most people make the mistake of always riding in too high a gear. They make their bicycling hard work. The gears, properly used, make it easier.

If you plan to go on long rides or want to get places in a hurry, a ten-speed bicycle is your best choice.

RACING BICYCLES

Because of its dropped or turned-under handlebars, the common ten-speed bicycle is mistakenly called a racing bicycle by many people. True, some of these bicycles are used in road races. But except for general appearance, the bicycles used for track racing are quite different. Custom built, they have no fenders (mudguards), no brakes, and a fixed gear. Each is geared to a specific speed or sprocket combination that is determined by the kind of race. The speed can be changed only by putting on different combinations of sprockets. To stop a track-racing bicycle, the racer back pedals and at the same time puts a gloved hand on the front wheel. A racing bicycle is stripped to only essential parts and has no accessories. The racer does not want to carry extra weight, and so anything that might hold down speed is eliminated. The slim tires on a racing bicycle are typically made of silk and are inflated to more than 100 pounds (45 kg) of pressure.

VARIATIONS

Several variations of these basic types of bicycles can be bought. Among the most popular today are small-wheeled bicycles that have long, slim seats ("banana" style) and high handlebars. Because of the way they are geared, these small bicycles are surprisingly easy to pedal. They have sturdy frames and are built to withstand quite a bit of abuse. Both trick bicycles and those used in playing the fast and exciting game of bicycle polo are very similar in design to these popular, small-wheeled bicycles, which are the sports cars of the bicycle world. Folding bicycles that can be stored in a

Left: racing bicycles on a slanted wooden track.
Above: this couple is riding a tandem bicycle.

PEPSI-COLA YOUTH SPORTS

small space or easily tucked into a car also have small wheels.

Among the other general types are tandems, or "bicycles built for two." These are fun to ride occasionally, and they may be the only way for a person who is blind or handicapped in some other way to be able to enjoy bicycling. Unicycles, which have a seat mounted over a single wheel, are also strictly for fun. Many older people ride giant-sized tricycles.

No matter what kind of bicycle you select, however, it is best to buy from a reputable dealer whose primary business is selling and servicing bicycles. Also buy a well-known brand. Many poorly made bicycles are on the market today, but even a well-made imported bicycle is no good if you cannot get parts when you need them. You should get a bicycle made by a manufacturer who backs up the product with guarantees and sells through dealers who provide good service. Avoid getting a bicycle kit and trying to assemble the bicycle yourself. Your bicycle should be completely assembled, adjusted, and ready to ride when you leave the store.

A bicycle marathon being led by unicyclists.

4

SIZE AND FIT

A bicycle that is the wrong size and not adjusted to fit is uncomfortable to ride and is also inefficient. You do not, for example, select a bicycle by the size of its wheels. The size of the frame is most important, and then you must also make other adjustments to make certain the bicycle fits you precisely for comfortable riding. Most dealers are helpful in helping you make the proper frame selection and then in making the fitting adjustments.

FRAME SIZE

To check the frame size on a boy's bicycle, straddle the bicycle with both feet on the ground. The frame's top tube should be close to the crotch but should not touch it. You can also get the proper size by measurement. Measure your inside leg—from your crotch down one leg to the ground. Then measure the bicycle from the top of the frame where the seat post slides into it to the center of the big sprocket where the pedals are attached. This distance should be 10 inches (25.4 cm) less than your inside leg measurement.

SADDLE ADJUSTMENT

Before you take the bicycle out of the shop, adjust the height of the saddle. First remove the saddle from the frame and make a mark on the post 2 inches (5 cm) or more from the bottom. When you have the saddle in its proper position, this mark should not show, for you need at least 2 inches (5 cm) or more of the seat post inside the frame for safe anchorage.

When the saddle is at its correct height, you will be in almost a standing-up or walking position when you are sitting on the seat. This means that, when you are pedaling with the ball of your foot on the pedal, your leg will be almost straight when the pedal is in its lowest position. If you have never ridden a bicycle with the seat at the proper height, this may seem at first to be too high—but do not lower it. One of the common mistakes is riding with the saddle too low, which is like trying to pedal while sitting in a chair. For quick trips, this may not be noticeable, but the strain becomes great after only a short distance.

The front or nose of the saddle should be about 2 inches (5 cm) behind a line that drops vertically to the middle of the hanger where the pedals are attached. The saddle should be level or tilted up slightly—never down.

PEPSI

HANDLEBAR HEIGHT

Adjust the height of the handlebars so that the stem or top is level with or only slightly lower than the top of the seat. If you are using dropped bars, this will put your body automatically in the most efficient position to pedal—about a 45-degree angle. It will also distribute your weight evenly over the bicycle frame. If you have standard handlebars, you will be sitting more upright, but your hands will rest on the grips without needing to stretch.

These are only the basic measurements and positions, of course. Movements of a fraction of an inch can make considerable difference in your comfort if you are riding long distances. You can make these minor shifts after you have ridden your bicycle for a while. And once you have ridden a bicycle that is perfectly adjusted to fit, you will find that even a short ride with an improper fit is as uncomfortable as wearing the wrong size shoes.

No matter what your size, your bicycle must be fit to suit you.

5

ACCESSORIES—SOME NEEDED, SOME NOT

At your bicycle shop you will see a wide assortment of extras, or accessories, that you can add to your bicycle. Do not be in a hurry about buying these items. Get only those that will serve a need. Remember that everything you add is more weight to be hauled or is something else that might rattle or need repair.

REFLECTORS

These are essential and are required by law. Your bicycle will be equipped with one or more reflectors when you buy it, but you may want to add more. A reflector makes you more visible both during the day and at night. For this reason, it is really difficult to get more than might be useful. You should have reflectors on the front, rear, and sides of your bicycle. Those that are a part of the pedal are especially good. You can also wear a jacket or a shoulder band of a reflective material. Anything you do to help yourself be seen is important.

SAFETY FLAGS

Some people equip their bicycles with bright flags that are mounted on rods 6 to 8 feet (1.8 to 2.4 m) tall. The rods fit into a bracket that may be attached either at the front or at the rear of the bicycle. Out on the road or in town traffic, these flags definitely call attention to a bicyclist—and particularly to groups of bicyclists.

Not everyone agrees that the flags are good, however. They sometimes get in the way when you are getting on or off the bicycle and can cause a fall if you are not careful. They add resistance, making it a bit more difficult to pedal if you are riding a long distance. Serious injuries have also resulted when the poles have broken off in accidents. You will have to consider these advantages and disadvantages of safety flags and make a personal decision whether a flag is best for you.

LIGHTS

Headlights are required by law for riding at night. If you ride at night only rarely, you probably will not need anything more than a bracket that will hold a flashlight. You can remove the flashlight when you are not riding. Avoid getting the shiny (but usually poorly made) lights that operate on batteries but are permanently attached to your handlebars. Most of these rust quickly, the batteries leak—and your money is wasted. A good generator (dynamo) light set is a wise investment if you ride at night a lot. The best are designed so that the light remains constant even when you slow down, and most also have flashing red lights at the rear. Generator (dynamo) lights do require wires. Make certain these are fastened securely to your bicycle frame to keep them out of the way.

LOCKS

If it is necessary to leave your bicycle untended even for a short time, you should have a lock. The most useful are hardened steel chains or cables encased in plastic and fastened with combination locks or with padlocks that open with a key. With these you can fasten the wheels and frame of your bicycle to a post, tree, or some other immovable object. If your bicycle wheels have quick-release hubs, you can also take off the front wheel and carry it with you as an extra precaution.

CYCLOMETER

Most people like to know how far they have ridden, and the mechanism for making this measurement is the cyclometer. You should get the size that fits your bicycle's wheel.

Above: a good headlight is a necessity for riding at night. Below: the best protection against theft is a lock and plastic-covered chain.

HUFFY

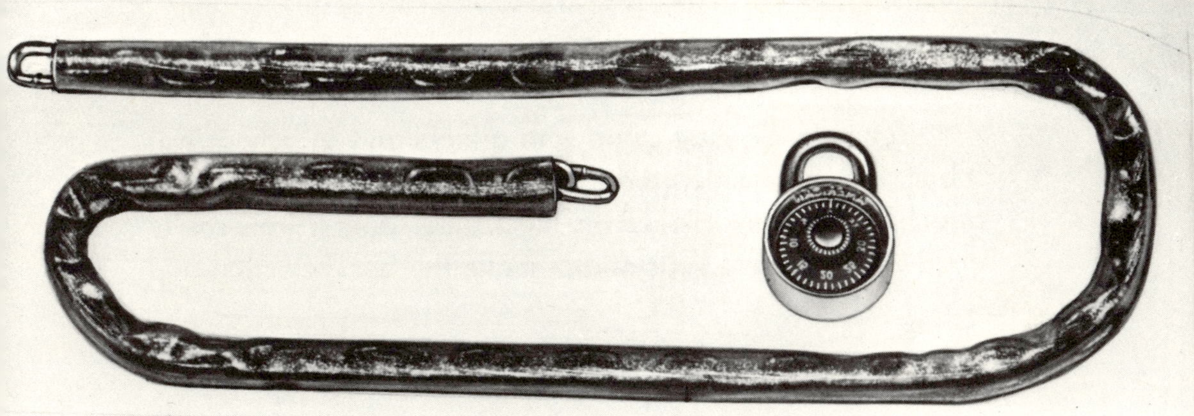

Your dealer can install the cyclometer for you, or by following the instructions in the box, you can do it yourself.

Speedometers are also available, but they seldom work well. New kinds are being developed, and you can ask your dealer to show you some and how they operate.

PUMP

If you take rides far from home and especially if you travel on country roads, it is wise to have a pump that fastens to the frame of your bicycle. These really do not operate very well, but in an emergency, they are greatly appreciated. At home you should definitely have a foot pump, preferably one with a gauge attached. Bicycle tires contain only a small volume of air under a high pressure, and so they must be filled often.

You can use the air pumps provided for cars at gas stations, but be extremely careful! The air is under very high pressure, and it is very easy to overinflate and explode your bicycle tires.

KICKSTAND

Your bicycle may come with a kickstand attached. If it is built into the frame, good. You can also buy kickstands to attach in different places on the frame, and if you really need a stand, have your dealer make the best selection and then fasten it in place for you. Kickstands have the unfortunate habit of working loose. Then they rattle and also get in the way when you pedal. And a kickstand that does not hold your bicycle securely and lets it fall is really worse than none at all.

Unless you have a very definite need for a kickstand, in fact, it is actually better to lean your bicycle against a building or a tree. Or you can lay it carefully on the ground—always with the chain side up to keep the dirt out.

CARRIERS AND BAGS

If you are carrying newspapers, you will probably need a big wire basket in front and maybe even large wire panniers on each side. For shopping, a wire basket in front may be all you need. For recreational rides, you will probably want a small handlebar bag. The kind supported with a metal holder is best. You can also get roomy saddlebags for longer trips, and if you plan a camping trip, pannier bags that hang down on each side of the rear wheel are available.

Some bicyclists' needs are satisfied with a small tool bag that hangs behind the saddle, or they may use only flat-topped metal carriers with a spring-clip clamping device. These carriers may be attached either at the front or the rear, and it is best to avoid those that must be anchored to the axle. They become a problem when a tire must be changed, and some also interfere with the operation of the wheel. Elastic

cords with plastic-covered hooks at their ends are very helpful in holding items on carriers or even to the frame.

OTHER ACCESSORIES

The kinds of things you can add to your bicycle are limitless. Again, be cautious. Get what you really need and will use, and avoid the temptation to buy gimmicks.

In some areas and countries you are required to have either a bell or a horn on your bicycle. A simple hand-operated bell is probably the most satisfactory. Avoid those that are operated with batteries.

Mirrors that fasten to handlebars are considered good by many bicyclists, but they are easily broken off if your bicycle falls. You can also get little mirrors that attach to sunglasses or to a cap, and there are wide-angle mirrors that are strapped to your hand. Mirrors are useful in some circumstances, but you should also learn how to look over your shoulder quickly without swerving.

Water bottles are valuable accessories for those who take long rides, especially in summer. Bicyclists may not notice that they are perspiring heavily because the sweat evaporates rapidly as they move through the air. But if the lost fluids are not replaced by drinking water or juice, a bicyclist soon becomes exhausted. Plastic water bottles are held in a

Bicycle baskets can be used to carry anything.

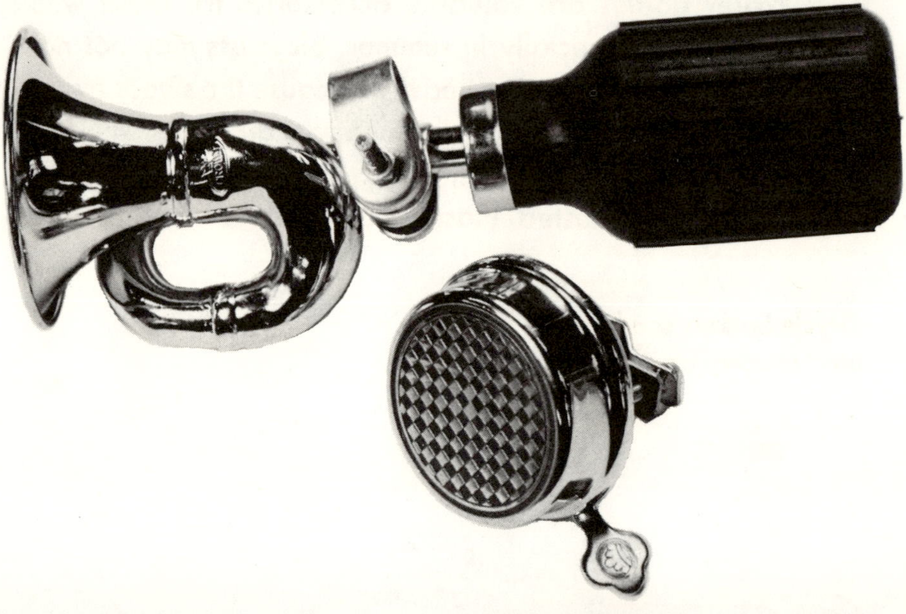

wire frame attached either to the handlebars or to the frame, or they can be carried in a touring bag.

Repellents for dogs, lightweight trailers, radios, crash helmets, gloves, special bicycling clothes and shoes—the list of accessories could go on and on. New items are added to the market almost every day. And what one person considers an essential may be strictly a gadget to somebody else. Most important is having a good basic bicycle. What you add to it is your business.

Above: an over-accessorized bicycle can be a hazard.
Below: a bicycle horn or bell—an important accessory.

6

TAKING CARE OF YOUR BICYCLE

When you get a new bicycle, you will find a folder or booklet attached to it. This will tell you how to take care of your vehicle to make it operate smoothly and last longer. If you read these instructions and then follow them, a good bicycle will literally last a lifetime and may need almost no replacement parts except tires.

PERIODIC INSPECTIONS

To keep your bicycle in good operating condition, you should give it a regular inspection—at least once a month or even more frequently if you ride often. Many bicyclists who really take pride in their machines give them a quick cleaning with a cloth after each ride. At the same time they can note whether spokes are loose, whether the tires are in good condition, and similar items that can be seen at a glance.

On a more thorough periodic examination, make certain that all nuts and bolts or screws are tight. Spin first the front wheel and then the rear wheel to make sure they revolve smoothly and without a wobble. If you have caliper brakes, examine the shoes that fit against the rim. They should not be more than a quarter of an inch (.6 cm) from the rim on each side, and if they are worn, they should be replaced. Also look at the cables that operate the brakes and the gears. They should move smoothly in their casings and should not be frayed or show signs of rust.

As you spin the wheels, let your fingers run over the spokes to check for looseness. Examine the seat post to be sure it is still tightly in place and has not shifted. Also inspect the handlebar stem. If grips or wrappings are badly worn, replace them. The pedals should spin freely (bent pedals are not uncommon) and should be securely screwed into the hangers. If you have pedals with rubber-block treads, they should not be excessively worn.

Look at the front fork and frame to make certain they are not bent. Check your chain and replace it if it is worn. Lubricate moving parts with a high-grade oil (not all-purpose) that you can buy from your bicycle dealer. But avoid using too much oil; a few drops every periodic check are sufficient. You can clean your chain with kerosene or a similar grease solvent, but use it carefully and sparingly. Either remove the chain, or if you leave it on the bicycle, take extreme care that the kerosene does not get on you or your tires. Use an old toothbrush to clean the grease and grit from between the sprockets. Wipe them clean and apply a very light coat of oil.

As you learn about your bicycle and how it operates, you will feel comfortable making more and more repairs and adjustments yourself. But if major work is necessary, it is really best to have your dealer do the work. A dealer is trained, experienced, and has the special tools needed for some kinds of repairs. People who ride their bicycles regularly have their machines completely serviced every six months.

7

GOOD AND SAFE RIDING

You can balance your bicycle, pedal and really go places. But are you a good bicyclist? Do you ride safely? What can you do to improve yourself?

PEDAL PROPERLY

Watch other people as they pedal, and you will see that some of them only push down every time a pedal comes up—first one side and then the other. And sometimes they push so hard they wobble or jerk from side to side. To pedal like this is hard work and not very efficient.

To pedal properly, you should follow through with each revolution of the pedals. In bicycling, this is called "ankling." As the pedal comes to the top in a revolution, you automatically drop your heel slightly and continue to apply pressure. When the pedal is midway down, your foot is almost level as you continue to push down, smoothly and without a jerky shove. When the pedal is in its down position, your heel is slightly lifted so that you help the pedal up the other side. Midway, your foot is nearly level as you are lifting up on the pedal.

Toe clips are a great help in achieving this follow-through or ankling movement. Full toe clips are fastened with a strap, which many people do not pull tight. If you have to do a lot of starting and stopping, getting your feet in and out of the toe clips each time can be a bother. You can get half-sized toe clips if the larger ones are inconvenient. But by all means, learn to pedal smoothly.

POSITION

On short rides, an erect or straight-backed position is satisfactory. You will not be riding far enough or long enough to have it be bothersome. If you do ride far, however, the "racing" position—that is, with your body at about a 45-degree angle—is by far the most comfortable and efficient. Your weight is distributed evenly over the frame of your bicycle, and you offer the least amount of resistance to the air. You also have better control of your bicycle for turning and are able to let your leg muscles apply maximum power to the pedals.

On long rides you will discover another advantage of the dropped or "racing style" handlebars. Rather than hav-

This man is using toe clips.

ing to hold your hands and arms in one position, which is necessary with standard handlebars, you can shift them into a variety of positions to give them a rest.

GEARING FOR COMFORT

Shifting gears properly is also important in good riding. As described in the discussion of the derailleur, you should avoid riding in too high a gear. First pedal at a rate that is most comfortable for you and that you can maintain without getting tired on a long ride. Shift to the gear that allows you to pedal at this rhythm with the greatest ease. With a bicycle, remember, you change gears by the "feel" of the riding conditions. Going from a lower to a higher gear does not mean that you will automatically go faster. Your muscles must supply the power for whatever speed you travel, but you use the gears to help you get where you want to go with the least amount of energy.

RULES OF THE ROAD

When you ride on streets and highways, you must obey the same laws as automobiles. You must also keep your wits about you at all times. If you tangle with an automobile or a truck, even if you are legally in the right, you will not be the winner. You and your bicycle are very fragile compared to motorized vehicles that weight a ton or more.

Always ride in the direction of the traffic and in a

straight line, without wavering or wobbling. Signal when turning, using the same hand signals that automobile drivers use. Stop at red or yellow traffic lights or stop signs. If you come to a busy intersection, walk your bicycle across. Be on the alert for cars pulling out of parking spaces, for suddenly opened doors, and for storm sewer gratings into which your wheel might slip and cause an upset. Never ride two on a bicycle or hitch rides by holding onto cars or trucks. In groups, ride in single file.

Find out if there are special regulations about bicycles where you live or where you plan to ride, and then obey them. For example, in some areas it is illegal to ride a bicycle on the pavement; in other areas, the pavement has been converted into bicycle paths, with the regulations insisting that you ride there.

SKILL TESTS

The best and most experienced bicyclists are continually checking their skills, just as any athlete keeps in practice in order to give the best possible performance.

Safe bicycle riding courses are now offered in many schools, or sometimes they are conducted by the police or local bicycle clubs. No matter how well you think you can ride, never miss an opportunity to have your skills tested at one of these courses.

The courses always start with an examination of your bicycle to see that it is in good operating condition. If you

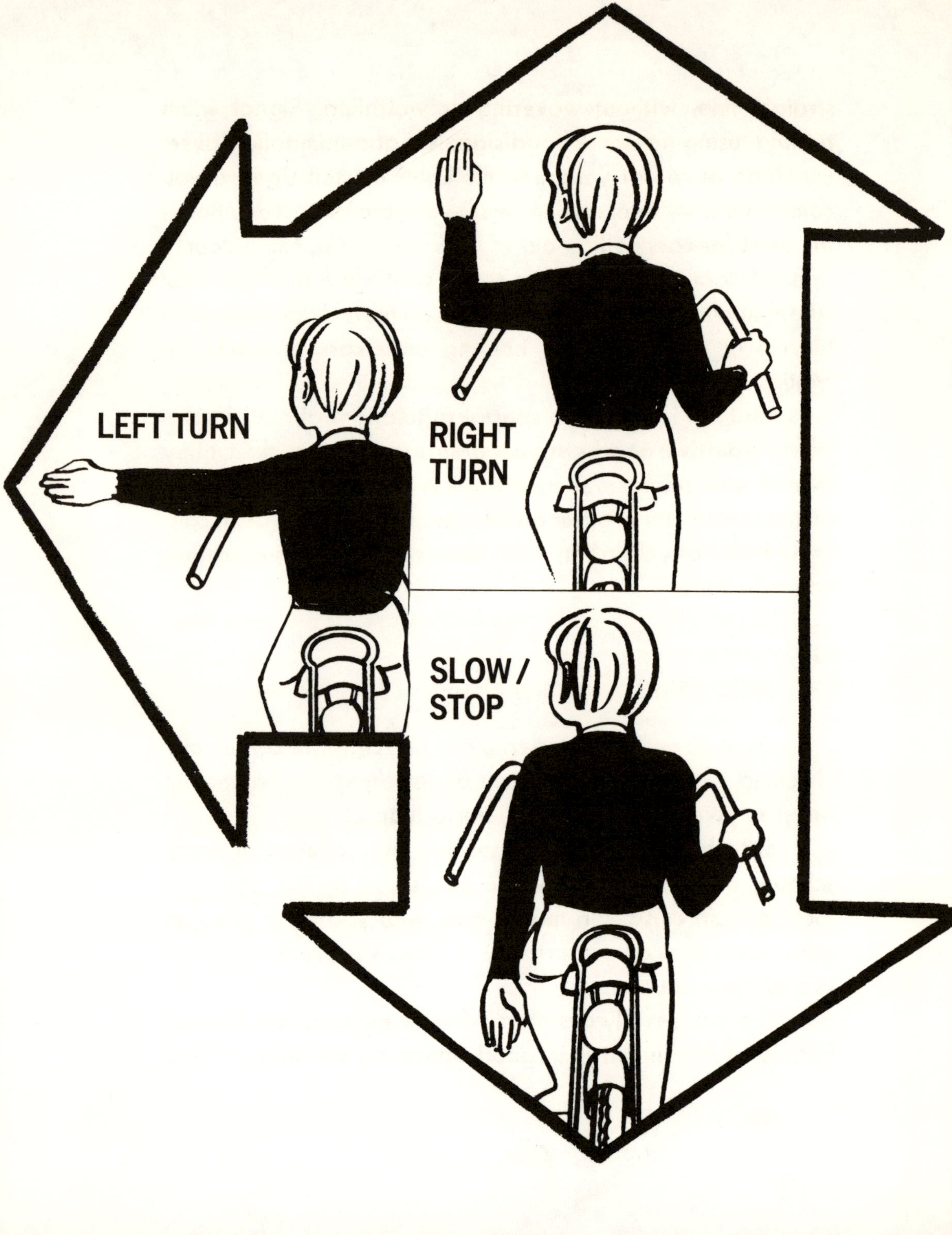
LEFT TURN
RIGHT TURN
SLOW / STOP

have been taking care of your bicycle properly, you can be proud when it is inspected. Besides, it is always good to have somebody else check your vehicle. The inspector might spot something you have been missing time after time. Remember, the check is for your safety.

Next you will probably be tested to see that you can start and stop smoothly. A weaving, wobbly start or stop in traffic is very dangerous. You start by straddling your bicycle with one foot on a pedal in its up position and the other foot on the ground. You glance over your shoulder to check the traffic, and if the way is clear, you push with your foot on the ground and at the same time push down on the pedal. Quickly you settle into the saddle, put your other foot on the free pedal and maintain your speed so that you move off without a wobble.

You stop by applying your brakes and at the same time stop pressing on your pedals. Just before your bicycle comes to a stop, you slide off the saddle so that your feet are on the ground. You make your stop without a wobble, staying in the straight line in which you have been riding.

In a test of riding skill, the examiners may have you ride 100 feet or more (30 m) on a course where there are two lines about 4 inches (10 cm) apart. You should be able to ride the full length with your wheels always between those lines. You may also be asked to make signals for right and left

Proper hand signals

turns while you are riding. This will demonstrate that you know the signals and also that you can keep on your course with only one hand on the handlebars.

During the sessions, you will be instructed on how to turn at a stop sign and an uncontrolled junction, how to move safely from a curb, and how to turn at traffic lights. You will also be shown the correct riding positions, and pedal and bicycle control.

To see how well you can ride in traffic situations, you will be asked to line up with several other bicyclists, the handlebars of your bicycles almost touching. At a signal, all of you should be able to start off together without hitting each other, and you should also be able to stop together.

Other tests will check your ability to make emergency stops, your skill at missing objects, and your ability to change directions smoothly. To test your ability to stop, you may be asked to ride rapidly toward a plank laid across your course and then to come to a full stop with your wheel almost touching the plank. Traffic cones, cans, milk cartons or similar objects will be placed at about 6-foot (2-m) intervals along a straight course, and then you will be asked to ride the course by going first to the right of one object and then to the left of the next—all without knocking over any of them. An examiner or two may stand along the course and then shout directions, telling one bicyclist to turn to the right, the next one to the left, or perhaps giving two rights—mixing up the directions to make sure you can change your course rapidly and smoothly.

Tests such as these will check the skill with which you handle your bicycle. You will also be expected to recognize standard traffic signs and to answer the same kinds of questions that automobile drivers are asked on their examinations. Legally, a bicycle is no different than an automobile, except your machine is powered by muscles and does not pollute. For fuel, you use eggs, milk, bread, meat, vegetables, and maybe now and then a big milk shake or a banana split. It's really a much better fuel system.

These are the kinds of tests you might be expected to pass in a bicycle course. They are really easy if you are a good bicycle rider. You and your friends can set up your own examination station in a vacant playground and then test your skills whenever you want to.

8

FUN AND GAMES

At a park, in a vacant playground, or wherever you can be totally away from automobile traffic, you can play games on bicycles with your friends. Most of the games also demand skill at handling your bicycle, and they are enjoyed by boys and girls, young and old.

SHIPWRECKED

This is like playing Pin the Tail on the Donkey, but you use your bicycle. In the middle of an open area, you make a big bull's-eye target. The outer ring can be 5 or 6 feet (1.5 or 1.8 m) in diameter, with rings a foot (30 cm) apart all the way to the middle or bull's-eye. A rider is blindfolded and given some object to put on the ground as close to the bull's-eye as possible. Before the blindfold is put in place, the rider may be given the opportunity to judge the distance to the bull's-eye. If there are teams, the contestant's teammates may be permitted to clap their hands to give a hint when the rider is getting close. Soft clapping, for example, may mean not very close. Louder clapping means closer. When the rider believes the bull's-eye is near, the bicycle is stopped, and the object is placed on the ground. Score is kept by allowing so many points for a bull's-eye and fewer points for each ring beyond the bull's-eye. Depending on the number of players, each may be allowed several turns before a tally is made to determine the winner.

Because the contestant is blindfolded and there may be much shouting, it is wise to have some sort of special signal, such as a whistle, to be used as a warning when a rider gets turned in the wrong direction and may be headed for danger. The whistle is a signal to stop.

HITTING THE TARGET

Put several coffee or similar-sized cans in a row about 15 feet (4.5 m) apart. Give each contestant some objects (pebbles, marbles, nuts, or similar items) and let them ride along a line drawn close to the cans. They are to see if they can drop an object into each can. If you have a group of riders, they can follow each other closely. Each rider can use a different kind of object, or if there are enough people, you can station scorers at the cans to record the number of hits.

Boys and girls who deliver newspapers like to use buckets and then throw folded newspapers into them. The line from which they throw can be put back far enough so that hitting the can compares to throwing a newspaper on a doorstep.

RIDING THE PLANK

Put planks (6 inches or 15 cm wide) on the ground end to end to make a lane of planks about 100 feet (30 m) long. If you have enough planks, you can make several of these lanes. A rider is started about 15 feet (4.5 m) from the end of a plank lane so that the bicycle has sufficient speed by the time the planks are reached. A contestant should be able to ride the full length of the plank lane without a wheel going off the plank. If you have several lanes, you can make it a racing event, starting the contestants for the different lanes at the same time. The winner can be the rider who gets to the end of the plank lane first without having gone off the course along the way. Or for a variation, the winner can be the one who gets there last.

BALLOON RACE

On a course 50 to 100 feet (15 to 30 m) long, place a number of balloons, anchoring them with strings tied to small rocks. If the course is 100 feet (30 m), you may have 10 balloons equally spaced. Riders are given 10 points for each balloon they break with their wheels as they ride toward the finish line. The one who goes over the finish line first gets 50 points. But a rider must decide which will get the most points: breaking more balloons or hurrying over the finish line.

PICK AND PUT

This is a popular event that tests the speed with which you can get off your bicycle and then back on it again. Make two circles about 10 feet (3 m) in circumference and roughly 50 feet (15 m) apart. Put half a dozen or more objects in one of the circles. The contestant starts at the empty circle and rides to the circle containing the objects, gets off the bicycle, picks up one object, then gets on the bicycle and brings it back to the empty circle. There the rider must dismount and deposit the object. This is repeated until all of the objects are moved to the empty circle. Time is recorded, and the one who moves all of the objects in the least time is declared the winner.

If you have enough contestants, you can make two sets of circles and then let the contestants race to see who gets all of the objects moved first. This can also be done with teams competing against each other.

SLOW RACE

This race is fun for everyone. The course should be about 100 feet (30 m) long and divided into several lanes about 5 feet (1.5 m) wide. At the starting signal, the racers head for the finish line, but it is the last one to get there who wins the race. A rider who gets out of a lane, touches a foot to the ground, or turns around is automatically out of the race. It requires great balancing skill to win this race.

FAST RACES

Fast races are fun, too. However, you should never race on the street unless it has been blocked off especially for a race. Bicycle races of this sort are popular in some towns and cities, with hundreds or even thousands of people lining the streets to watch the racers. In some areas there are also special tracks for bicycle racing, and more are being built every year.

In real road races, the distances may be 100 or even 200 miles (160 to 320 km) for a day's event, and the racers will average about 25 miles (40 km) per hour. The most famous of all road races is the Tour de France in which the racers travel about 2500 miles (4000 km) in 26 or 27 days.

Track races are held on banked tracks or velodromes, and the racers may travel at speeds of 50 miles (80 km) per hour or even faster in sprints. Some of the sprint races are only about half a mile (.8 km) long. Other races may be for 50 miles (80 km) or more. Six-day races on tracks were once very popular in the United States and are still held in Canada and in Europe.

Bicycle racing is a great sport. In many countries, bicycle racers are higher paid than are any other athletes. The interest in bicycle racing is growing everywhere.

9

RIDES AND TOURS

On your bicycle, you can ride down the street or around the world. You can ride alone, or you can join a group. And it is a great feeling to be able to go where you want whenever you wish, supplying your own power.

GROUP RIDES

Except for local rides, it is best to go with a group, not only for safety but also because it is more fun. In almost every town and city today, there is a bicycle club. It consists of a group of people who are just as interested in bicycling as you are. If you want to go on rides and tours with company, join the club. You will also get all of the various club benefits.

Youth Hostels often conduct all kinds of tours in which the participants must travel by muscle power. This includes bicycling, of course. Some of the tours are in your own country, others in foreign countries. A letter to the Youth

Hostel Association will bring you a brochure describing its facilities and listing its local branches. One may be near you.

In the beginning, a ride of 5 or 10 miles (8 or 16 km) may seem like a big adventure to you. Later you may think nothing of riding 100 miles (160 km) in a day. On some of your rides, the bicycling itself is the primary focus. On others you may be using your bicycle as a means of transportation to some park or other place of interest. No matter what you have as an objective, do some careful planning ahead of time. Let someone know where you are going and when you can be expected to return. In a special place, always carry with you an identification card and a few coins for making a telephone call. Do not use this money for any other purpose. If you are delayed or have some sort of problem along the road, you will have money to call for help.

On rides of any length, always carry a few tools with you to take care of minor repairs. All the tools you will need can be put in a little tool bag that fastens behind your saddle, or can be tucked into a front touring bag or larger saddlebag, depending on what you have. The basic items that will take care of almost all of the problems you might have are a small screwdriver, a small adjustable wrench, a small pair of pliers, a tire repair kit (this will include instructions), a folding knife, one or two tire tools, a roll of plastic tape, and a spoke wrench. You may also want to add a cog remover, a brake cable, a derailleur cable, and a chain tool. Some riders take several extra spokes with them. They can be fastened to the frame of your bicycle with tape. If you have

Riding in groups can be a fun way to see the sights.

No matter where you go, you will find other bicyclists ready to join you.

problems that cannot be fixed with these tools, it is best to get your bicycle to the nearest repair shop.

When you are on a long ride, you can decide ahead of time where you will be stopping for food. This may be at a restaurant—or you may either carry a lunch with you or stop and buy the "makings" for a picnic. Bicycling does take a lot of fuel, and so you will be wise to carry snack items with you. Apples, oranges, and bananas are excellent. Some bicyclists take with them a bag of raisins, peanuts, and chocolate bits mixed together. This is a high-energy concoction that is also tasty.

TOURS

If you go on overnight trips or tours that last for a week or longer, you will work out ahead of time the details of the route and what you should carry. The leader should be a person who has taken such trips before, and you can benefit from this person's experience if this is a first time for you.

On some tours you will be staying overnight in motels or other lodging places. You will travel light, and all of your needs can be stowed in a front touring bag and a big saddlebag. On some camping trips, the sleeping bags, cooking gear, and other such items are transported from one camping area to the next by automobile or van so that the bicyclists are not burdened. On other trips, each bicyclist must carry everything needed. This requires big, hanging pannier bags on either side of the rear wheel. Balance and steering are greatly affected by these heavy loads. If you do plan such an excursion, you should equip your bicycle with its load and then take a few short-distance trial rides to get the "feel" of handling your vehicle when it is loaded. You can also do some practice loading and unloading and perhaps discover ahead of time what items you have forgotten or what you can leave behind to help keep the load as light as possible.

But wherever you want to go, no matter how short or how far the ride, you will find other bicyclists ready to join you. In the summer of 1976, for example, more than four thousand bicyclists pedaled from coast to coast across the United States as part of the Bicentennial celebration. They were "trailblazing" bicycle routes. They left marked trails and have added more since then as they have continued to cobweb the country with safe and scenic routes for fellow bicyclists to follow.

SUGGESTED READING AND BICYCLING ORGANIZATIONS

SUGGESTED READING

Ballantine, Richard: *Richard's Bicycle Book*. New York: Ballantine Books, 1972.

Browder, Sue: *The American Biking Atlas and Touring Guide*. New York: Workman Publishing Co., 1974.

Kingbay, Keith: *Inside Bicycling*. Chicago: Regnery, 1976.

Kleeberg, Irene: *Bicycle Repair*. New York: Franklin Watts, 1973.

———: *Bicycle Touring*. New York: Franklin Watts, 1975.

Sloane, Eugene A: *Complete Book of Bicycling*. New York: Trident Press, 1970.

Smith, Robert A.: *A Social History of the Bicycle*. New York: American Heritage Press, 1972.

Wagenvoord, James: *Bikes and Riders*. New York: Van Nostrand Reinhold Company, 1972.

BICYCLING ORGANIZATIONS

American Youth Hostels, National Campus, Delaplane, Virginia 22025. Tours.

League of American Wheelmen, 19 South Bothwell, Palatine, Illinois 60067. Tours and general recreational riding.

United States Cycling Federation, P.O. Box 480, East Detroit, Michigan 48021. Racing.

INDEX

ABOUT THE AUTHOR

George S. Fichter has had a varied professional career, which includes his having been a college instructor of zoology and conservation, editor-in-chief of Fisherman Press, and author of more than 300 magazine articles and over three dozen books. Mr. Fichter and his wife, Nadine, originated and developed the Bikeways concept now widely used in the United States, for which they received a national award from American Youth Hostels. They live in Homestead, Florida.